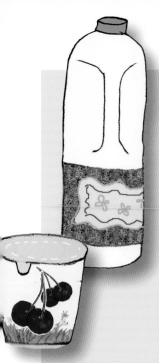

Healthy Eating

Milk Butter and Cheese

Susan Martineau
and Hel James

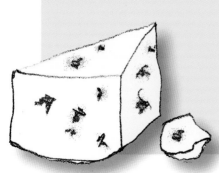

A⁺
Smart Apple Media

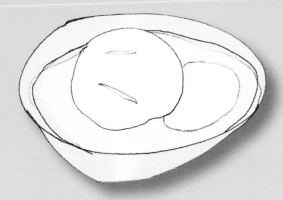

Published by Smart Apple Media
2140 Howard Drive West, North Mankato, MN 56003

Designed and illustrated by Helen James
Edited by Jinny Johnson

Printed in Thailand

Library of Congress Catalog-in-Publication Data

Martineau, Susan.
Healthy eating. Milk, butter, and cheese / by Susan Martineau.
p. cm.
Includes index.
ISBN-13: 978-1-58340-895-7
1. Dairy products—Juvenile literature. I. Title. II. Title: Milk, butter, and cheese.

TX377.M37 2006
641.3'7—dc22   2006008871

First Edition
9 8 7 6 5 4 3 2 1

Contents

Food for health

Our bodies are like amazing machines.
Just like machines, we need the right
kind of fuel to give us energy and
to keep us working properly.

If we don't eat the kind of food we need to keep us healthy, we may become ill or feel tired and grumpy. Our bodies do not like it if we eat too much of one kind of food, such as cakes or chips.

We need a balanced diet. That means eating different kinds of good food in the right amounts.

You'll be surprised at how much there is to know about where our food comes from and why some kinds of food are better for us than others. Finding out about food is great fun and very tasty!

I feel like a milkshake.

My favorite is strawberry.

Milk, yogurt, and cheese help us to build strong bones and teeth.

A balanced meal!

The good things, or **nutrients**, our bodies need come from different kinds of food. Let's look at what your plate should have on it. It all looks delicious!

Rice, bread, and pasta

These foods contain **carbohydrates** and they give us energy. They are also called starchy foods. About a third of our food should come from this group.

Fruits and vegetables

Rice, bread, and pasta

Bread, cheese, and salad give you carbohydrates, protein, vitamins, and minerals.

6

Fruits and vegetables

These are full of great **vitamins**, **minerals**, and **fiber**. They do all kinds of useful jobs in your body to help keep you healthy. About a third of our food should come from this group.

Milk, yogurt, and cheese

These dairy foods give us protein and **calcium** to make strong bones and teeth.

Meat, fish, and eggs

Protein from these helps your body grow and repair itself. They are body-building foods. You should eat some of them every day.

Sugar and fats

Eat only small amounts of these. Too much can be bad for our teeth and make us overweight.

Milk, yogurt, and cheese

Sugar and fats

Meat, fish, and eggs

Water

We need to drink at least six glasses of water every day.

Dairy goodness

Dairy foods are made from milk. They include yogurt, cheese, butter, and cream. Dairy foods give us body-building protein and calcium. Calcium is very good for us and helps us to grow strong bones and teeth.

We need some calcium every day. Eating milk, yogurt, and cheese is the best way to get calcium. Cream and butter have a lot of fat in them so they belong in the sugar and fats part of the balanced meal. Our bodies only need a little bit of fat.

Bone-building menu

Breakfast

Pour some milk on your breakfast cereal.

Calcium helps to keep your teeth healthy.

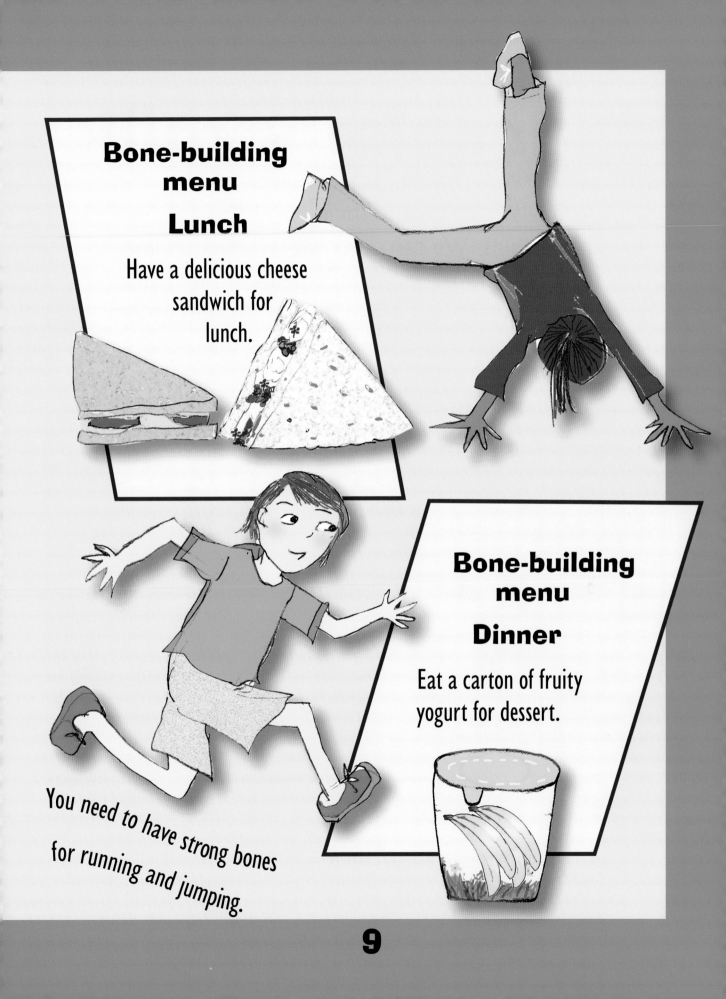

Bone-building menu
Lunch

Have a delicious cheese sandwich for lunch.

Bone-building menu
Dinner

Eat a carton of fruity yogurt for dessert.

You need to have strong bones for running and jumping.

Marvelous milk

Animals make milk in their own bodies to feed their babies. We can drink the milk that animals make, too. Most of the milk people drink comes from cows. You can also drink milk from goats, sheep, buffalo, and even reindeer!

This calf will grow big and strong from its mother's milk.

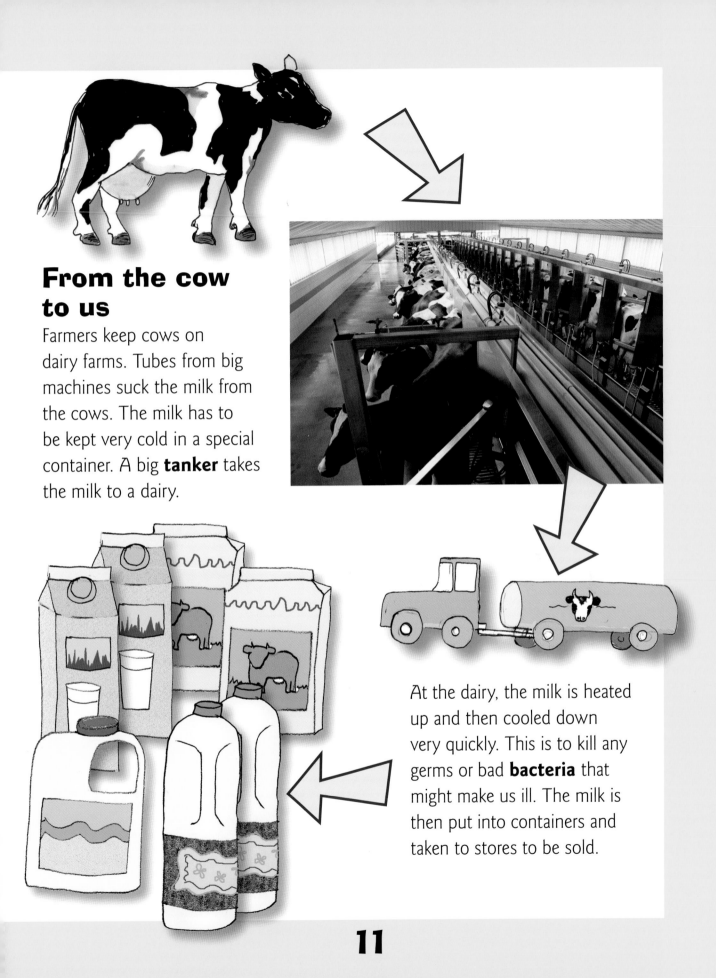

From the cow to us

Farmers keep cows on dairy farms. Tubes from big machines suck the milk from the cows. The milk has to be kept very cold in a special container. A big **tanker** takes the milk to a dairy.

At the dairy, the milk is heated up and then cooled down very quickly. This is to kill any germs or bad **bacteria** that might make us ill. The milk is then put into containers and taken to stores to be sold.

Kinds of milk

Milk has fat in it and the fat is what we call cream. Before the milk is put into containers at the dairy, it is **processed**, or made into different kinds of milk, with more or less fat in it.

Pancakes are a delicious way to use milk!

What about organic milk?

Some people think that **organic** milk is better for us. Cows producing organic milk eat grass that has not been sprayed with **chemicals** to kill bugs and weeds.

Make the most of milk

Milk is a healthy drink full of nutrients for your body. You can use milk in lots of other great ways, too.

Whole milk has all the fat left in it.

Low-fat milk has about half the fat taken out of it.

Skim milk has all the fat taken out of it.

Whole and low-fat milk are the best for young, growing bodies.

13

Special milks

Some people cannot drink cow's milk or eat the dairy foods made from it. They are **allergic** to it, and it makes them feel sick. Other people just don't like the taste of milk!

Luckily, you can still get protein and calcium from other kinds of milk, like the milk from goats and sheep. There is also milk made from soy beans and rice. Calcium and vitamins are added to it to make it a healthy choice. Soy milk can also be made into yogurt and cheese.

Next time you are in a food store, look at the different types of milk you can buy. It's nice to know that even if you are allergic to cow's milk, there are lots of other bone-building choices!

Whip up a milkshake using your favorite soft fruit, like strawberries or bananas, with any kind of milk you like. Just put everything in a blender or food processor and mix it well. Slurp it up!

- a big cup of milk
- a handful of fruit
- 2 tablespoons of ice cream

All kinds of cream

The fat in milk floats to the top. You can sometimes see this in containers of whole or low-fat milk. This fat is called cream.

You can get many kinds of cream at the stores.

When cows have been milked, the cream can be skimmed off the top of the containers of milk. Like the milk, it must be heated up, or **pasteurized**, to kill any bad bacteria. After this, it also needs to be kept very cold to keep it fresh.

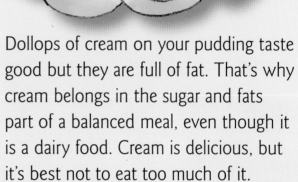

Dollops of cream on your pudding taste good but they are full of fat. That's why cream belongs in the sugar and fats part of a balanced meal, even though it is a dairy food. Cream is delicious, but it's best not to eat too much of it.

You can whisk cream into stiff peaks.

Yogurt

Yogurt is made from milk. It can be made from cow's milk or the milk from sheep, goats, and other animals. Yogurt can also be made from soy milk. Some harmless bacteria are added to the milk. Then it is heated up and left for a few hours before being cooled. It is put into containers ready for the stores.

Yogurt is as high or low in fat as the type of milk used to make it. It can be used instead of cream in all kinds of sweet and salty dishes.

Check for sugar

There are many different kinds of yogurt in the stores—plain, fruity, low-fat, and thick and creamy. But some kinds have lots of sugar in them, so check the labels before you buy them.

Yogurt tastes great on a pile of fresh fruit.

Yogurt with cucumber and mint is cooling and delicious with spicy food.

+ =

Butter and margarine

Butter is made out of cream. The cream is heated to kill any bad or harmful bacteria. Then it is put into large, revolving containers that beat and turn it. This makes all of the lumps of fat in it stick together and turn into butter! Like cream, butter has a lot of fat in it, and we should only eat small amounts.

Butter is churned until it is solid. Then it can be
cut into pieces, packaged, and sold.

Spreads for bread

Margarine is made out of different kinds
of vegetable oils. The oils are processed,
or "changed," into something we can
spread on our bread by mixing them with
special chemicals. This often makes a
kind of fat which is not very good for us.

All about oils

Oils are used to cook food or to make salad dressings and mayonnaise. Look at all of the different kinds of oils on the shelves in the supermarket. Some are made from seeds, like sunflower oil or corn oil.
Can you find any oils made from nuts?

Olive oil

Walnut oil

Sunflower oil

Corn oil

Of all the oils, olive oil is best for us. It is made from olives and tastes delicious in salad dressings.

Olives grow on trees. They are picked by hand or with special rakes.
The oil is then pressed out of them.

Know your fats!

Oils are called **unsaturated** fats
and they are not as bad for us as
fats like butter and cream. Butter
and cream are called **saturated**
fats. We do need a little bit of
fat to help our bodies to use
vitamins, but it is better to choose
unsaturated fats.

Cheese please!

Cheese is another dairy food. It can be made from cow's milk or the milk from other animals like goats or sheep. First, the milk is mixed with special bacteria. Then, another ingredient called **rennet** is added and this makes the milk into solid lumps called **curds**.

The curds are cut, shaped, and pressed to make all kinds of cheeses. Some cheeses are then kept for weeks or even months before being taken to the shops to be sold. This is called **ageing** the cheese.

Most cheese contains a lot of fat but it also gives our bodies protein, calcium, and vitamins.

Some cheeses smell very strong, but they still taste delicious.

Choosing cheese

There are lots of cheeses to choose.
Make a cheese quiz for your friends to find
out which type is their favorite.

Hard cheeses

These cheeses are aged for a few weeks
or months before being sold in the shops.
They are great in sandwiches for your
lunchbox or for making tasty cheese sauces
for vegetables or pasta.

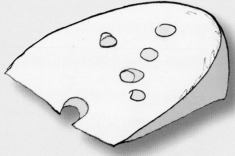

Swiss cheese is from Switzerland.
It has holes in it!

Parmesan is an Italian
cheese that is
delicious with
many kinds of
pasta dishes.

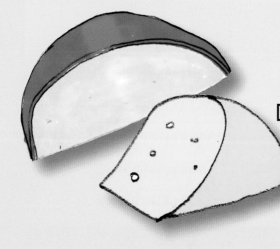

Dutch cheeses, such as Edam and Gouda,
have a special wax on the outside to
help keep them soft and fresh.

Cheeses have to be kept at just the right temperature when they are ageing.

Blue cheeses

These cheeses are made by adding harmless bacteria or mold to them. It sounds strange but they are very tasty. Try them with bread or crackers or stir some into soup.

Roquefort is a French cheese made from sheep's milk.

Stilton is a traditional English cheese.

Soft cheeses

Most soft cheeses do not keep for as long as hard cheeses. Soft cheeses, such as Camembert and Brie, do not need to be aged and should be eaten quite quickly.

Tubs of soft cheese

There are many different types of white soft cheese to spread on your bread. It is best to choose ones that are labeled "low-fat."

Trick cheese!

Fromage frais is usually put on the shop shelves next to yogurts but it is really a kind of soft cheese. It was first made in France. "Fromage frais" means "fresh cheese" in French.

Mozzarella is made from cow's or buffalo's milk and is great for pizzas. It comes in the shape of a ball and needs to be kept in water.

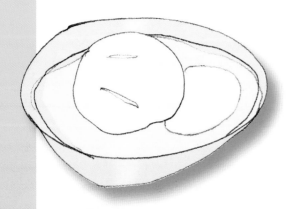

Camembert and Brie are made in France.

Words to remember

ageing   Keeping cheese for weeks or months before it is sold.

allergic   This means that you feel sick or get a rash or an upset stomach if you eat certain foods.

bacteria   Tiny creatures that are so small we cannot see them. Some bacteria are bad for us and can make us ill. Some bacteria do not hurt us and can be used to make yogurt and cheese. The bacteria in yogurt are good for our stomachs.

calcium   A mineral that helps build healthy bones and teeth.

carbohydrates   Starches and sugars in food that give us energy. Carbohydrate foods are rice, pasta, bread, and potatoes.

chemicals   Substances that can be used for many kinds of things. Some, called pesticides, are used to kill weeds in fields. Some chemicals are used to process food.

curds   The solid lumps that form when milk is being made into cheese.

dairy   Foods that contain milk, such as yogurt, cheese, butter, and cream, or a place where milk products are made.

fiber   Plant foods like grains and vegetables contain fiber. It helps our insides work properly.

low-fat milk   Milk that has had about half the fat taken out of it.

minerals   Nutrients in food that help our bodies work properly. Calcium is a mineral.

nutrients   Parts of food that your body needs to make energy, to grow healthily, and to repair itself.

organic   Grown without using chemicals to kill weeds and bugs. Organic milk comes from cows that eat grass that is not sprayed with chemicals.

pasteurized   When milk is heated to kill any bad bacteria that could make us ill.

processed   Foods that are processed go through some changes before they reach your plate. Oils are processed to make margarine.

rennet   Rennet helps to make the solid curd in cheese-making. Some rennet comes from the stomach of a calf. Rennet from plants is used to make vegetarian cheese.

saturated   Saturated fat is found in cream, butter, and cheese as well as in fatty meat.

skim milk   Milk that has had all the fat taken out of it.

tanker   Truck that has a large tank on it to keep milk cold while it is being taken to the dairy.

unsaturated   The sort of fat that is found in vegetable oils. It is also found in nuts, seeds, and oily fish.

vitamins   Nutrients in food that help our bodies work properly.

whole milk   Milk with all the cream left in it.

Index

Web sites

Learn which foods make a healthy heart.
http://www.healthyfridge.org/

Test your nutritional knowledge with quizzes, dietary guidelines, and a glossary of terms.
http://www.exhibits.pacsci.org/nutrition/

Find out how to have a healthy diet without eating meat.
http://www.vrg.org/family/kidsindex.htm

Get the facts about fast food restaurants and tips for making healthy choices.
http://library.thinkquest.org/4485/

Take the 5-a-day challenge and learn about fruits and vegetables with puzzles, music, and games.
http://www.dole5aday.com/

Discover ten tips for a healthy lifestyle.
http://www.fitness.gov/10tips.htm